Sound

WINNER OF THE 2020 DEBORAH TALL
LYRIC ESSAY BOOK PRIZE
Selected by Jenny Boully

DEBORAH TALL LYRIC ESSAY
BOOK PRIZE SERIES EDITORS
Geoffrey Babbitt and David Weiss

Like

Trapped

JESSICA LIND PETERSON

Thunder

SENECA REVIEW BOOKS

Published by Seneca Review Books, an imprint

of Hobart & William Smith Colleges Press

300 Pulteney St., Demarest 101

Geneva, NY 14456

www.hws.edu/senecareview

Seneca Review Books is grateful to Hobart & William Smith Colleges,

Hobart & William Smith Colleges Press, *Seneca Review*, and the

TRIAS Writer-in-Residence Program for their generous support.

ISBN: 978-0-910969-06-2

LCCN: 2020945359

Designed by Crisis

Printed in Michigan

Thank you to the following journals, where these essays first appeared (sometimes in different versions): "That Far North" (under the title "Strange Season")
in *Orion*; "This Is Doris Ronn" in *Alaska Quarterly Review*; "Beat a Dead" in
Seneca Review; "The Seahorse Difference" in *Anomaly* (formerly *Drunken Boat*);
and "The Little Girl, Her Drunk Bastard Parents, and the Hummingbird" in
Passages North. Some names and identifying details have been changed.

FOR J, W, & W

Deep in the forest there's an unexpected clearing which can be reached only by someone who has lost [their] way.

TOMAS TRANSTRÖMER

When I was six I tried to sleep every night with my arms folded behind my back like wings. This didn't last long, because it is very hard to sleep with your arms folded behind your back like wings.

HELEN MACDONALD

THE LITTLE GIRL, HER DRUNK BASTARD PARENTS, AND THE HUMMINGBIRD

A little girl with reddish brownish hair and big feet sat in a tree house in her backyard. The tree house was situated on the ground next to the garage, not up in a tree like you were thinking, and the tree house was made of wood from the rotting back porch as the little girl's father was a railroad worker, and railroad workers do not have special access to wood scraps like construction workers do. Also notable, the tree house had no roof and no walls, which made things sunny and fresh-smelling like dirt and apple blossoms and leaves and garages. The no roof/no walls detail will come in handy during the part where I tell you that a hummingbird flies into the tree house, because if I told you that a hummingbird flies into a tree house that *did* have a roof/walls you might think the hummingbird would have died on impact. I'm only trying to save you from despair.

In the little girl's hands was a round piece of wood which held a white piece of cloth which held a cross-stitch pattern of bright summer flowers which was very pretty indeed, though the stems on the flowers were a little bit crooked but so was the floor of the tree house

1

and that certainly may have had something to do with it. The little girl was briefly paused in her work because she felt like something was missing in her pretty scene of crooked flowers and so she needed to think about it. She always thought best when she was in her tree house so this was all very convenient. And speaking of conveniences, the thinking break came at a good time because the needle had caused a major indent on the end of her right index finger and she had put it in her mouth to soothe it. Let's just call it what it was — a sewing injury. (Her grandmother had told her this might happen. Her grandmother cross-stitched and also baked bread that the little girl was very fond of. Sometimes, she ate a whole half of a loaf right out of the oven with butter and raspberry jam and it ruined her dinner, but her grandmother let her and that is why this grandmother was her very favorite grandmother out of all her grandmothers. Also, the other grandmother always made the little girl sit in her great big lap and pluck the wiry black hairs from her chin with a tweezers. Gross, but also a nice challenge on Sundays. There was love there but a favorite grandmother is a favorite grandmother and no one on planet Earth can argue with that kind of sound logic. Her favorite grandmother was especially important these days since her father was a drunk bastard and her mother was on her way to becoming a drunk bastard. These are strong words but these are strong times. At first, it was just wine. Lots and lots of red wine. Her grandmother came to stay for two weeks and discovered a gargantuan number of wine bottles in the recycling bin and also two opened bottles in the unused basement sauna under an old ten-gallon paint bucket. After her grandmother confronted her mother about all those wine bottles two things happened. One, the mother began putting empty wine bottles into the neighbor's recycling bins very early in the morning on the day of recycling pickup. Two, the mother began drinking 7 and 7s with Canadian Club because it worked faster and that is what the drunk bastard father drank and Canada is not far away so it's good to support our border friends. If the grandmother said anything about the whiskey bottles the mother could just blame the father—badda bing, badda boom. It actually worked because even though the little girl told her grandmother that the mother was still doing weird, drunk bastard-type things like burning her arm so badly while taking a roast out of the oven that the fabric from her Christmas sweater actually became scorched into her skin like a tattoo, hiding her glass of booze behind picture frames in the early afternoons, talking to the little girl, who was thirty-eight years old, in a baby voice as if she were a toddler, and also forgetting her birthday all the time—her grandmother dismissed it, saying that perhaps the mother didn't want to get rings on the important parts of the coffee table and she was just being considerate of the furniture.)

Just so we're clear here. Two drunk bastard parents, one nice grandmother who is good at baking.

The little girl sat on the hard wooden floor of the tree house sucking on her sore finger, thinking about fresh bread and what else might go into her scene of crooked summer flowers and you'll never guess what happened next. The little girl started drinking whiskey too because fuck it, she liked the way it burned her throat just the right way and life was sad and hard and her husband had made a mistake exactly two years prior and she was having a difficult time with forgiveness and one or two drinks at night didn't mean she was turning into a drunk bastard, for crying out loud it's not like she's going to put a gun to her head while standing on the shores of Lake Superior in the middle of the afternoon in front of a pastor and his wife celebrating their wedding anniversary like her pretty, drunk aunt with a developing interest in crystals who was only fifty years old had just done. Gawd.

Anyway. A hummingbird flew right into the tree house and landed on the uneven wooden floor in a small, feathery thump. A thump so quiet, it barely registered on any super-secret seismic sound scale that was or was not recording backyard sound waves in that particular part of the Midwest. So quiet, it could have been a damp dandelion puff. Or a snip of overgrown bangs floating to the floor. Or a large ladybug landing. The little girl picked up the hummingbird and held it very carefully in her hand (the one without the gruesome sewing injury) and the first thing she thought was that this hummingbird was certainly a goner. One translucent wing motored hopelessly against her palm, the other one was tucked and still against its feathered thumb of breast. Its tongue, a lolling pink string, hung from the end of its needle beak. So tired and such a goner was this hummingbird, that it could not even reel its own tongue back in. Sad, but understandable. Circumstances were dire.

The little girl knew she should carry the hummingbird outside, set it in the grass and walk away, but that is not what she did. She just couldn't. She had a real dying fairy on her hands and she wanted to keep looking. The hummingbird glowed in the sunlight, green and red and neon, a tiny shimmering flag of itself. Nothing had ever been sadder or more beautiful at the same time. Not even a wet horse. Not even an orphaned baby elephant. Not even old roses. The little girl began to cry because to not cry was impossible. She felt so bad for this hummingbird who was clearly dying. It should be whirring above the tree house in blissful fits of motion. A mini, slick speed skater ripping through its track of air, magic in its fastness. To hold it, the little girl knew, was wrong. But it did not belong on the ground either. What would a hummingbird do with a sidewalk? Or sidewalk chalk for that matter? And she didn't want to put something so fragile as a one-winged hummingbird in the path of a drunk bastard mother who trips and falls on sidewalks and bruises three ribs while babysitting her three-year-old grandson. Uh-uh. No way. She did not want that on her reddish-brownish head.

The little girl decided that continuing to sit there in the tree house while holding the hummingbird in her noninjured hand seemed like the best plan for now. Though that plan faintly resembled doing nothing, she wasn't going to beat herself up about it. She was comfortable holding birds. Always had been. When she was an even littler girl, she had a pet parakeet named Blinkie who was blue and white and blinked a lot in accordance with his name. Every day after school the little girl would engage in intense training sessions with Blinkie. First, she taught him to fly directly from his cage to her finger. Then she taught him to crawl from her finger all the way up to her shoulder. Then she taught him to sleep on her bedpost at night. She loved Blinkie and Blinkie did or did not love her back. It's tough to tell with pet birds. They have that bird look, like, *I'm just looking at you to gather some information here. I like birdseed. Sitting on your finger is fine. Just keep the fucking golden retriever in the living room and I'll be your little friend.*

It was a relationship that just worked.

The one thing the little girl could never get Blinkie to do was talk. It's not that she didn't like his sweet garbly goos. She totally did. But she longed for some real conversation. Some actual words. Some tête-à-tête. So she bought a record at the Goodwill called *Teach Your Parrot to Talk* and played it every day after school, sometimes over and over again. Here is an example of what the record sounded like:

Hello. Hello. Hello. Hello. Hello. Hello. Hello. Hello. Hello.

Hello. Hello. Hello. Hello. Hello. Hello. Hello. Hello. Hello.

Hello. Hello. Hello. Hello. Hello. Hello. Hello. Hello. Hello.

Hello. Hello. Hello. Hello. Hello. Hello. Hello. Hello. Hello.

Hello. Hello. Hello. Hello. Hello. Hello. Hello. Hello. Hello.

Hello. Hello. Hello. Hello. Hello. Hello. Hello. Hello. Hello.

Hello. Hello. Hello. Hello. Hello. Hello. Hello. Hello. Hello.

Hello. Hello. Hello. Hello. Hello. Hello. Hello. Hello. Hello.

Hello. Hello. Hello. Hello. Hello. Hello. Hello. Hello. Hello.

Hello. Hello. Hello. Hello. Hello. Hello. Hello. Hello. Hello.

Hello. Hello. Hello. Hello. Hello. Hello. Hello. Hello. Hello.

Hello. Hello. Hello. Hello. Hello. Hello. Hello. Hello. Hello.

Hello. Hello. Hello. Hello. Hello. Hello. Hello. Hello. Hello.

Hello. Hello. Hello. Hello. Hello. Hello. Hello. Hello. Hello.

Hello. Hello. Hello. Hello. Hello. Hello. Hello. Hello. Hello.

Hello. Hello. Hello. Hello. Hello. Hello. Hello. Hello. Hello.

Hello. Hello. Hello. Hello. Hello. Hello. Hello. Hello. Hello.

(Next track.)

Pretty bird. Pretty bird. Pretty bird. Pretty bird. Pretty bird.

Pretty bird. Pretty bird. Pretty bird. Pretty bird. Pretty bird.

Pretty bird. Pretty bird. Pretty bird. Pretty bird. Pretty bird.

Pretty bird. Pretty bird. Pretty bird. Pretty bird. Pretty bird.

Pretty bird. Pretty bird. Pretty bird. Pretty bird. Pretty bird.

Pretty bird. Pretty bird. Pretty bird. Pretty bird. Pretty bird.

Pretty bird. Pretty bird. Pretty bird. Pretty bird. Pretty bird.
Pretty bird. Pretty bird. Pretty bird. Pretty bird. Pretty bird.
Pretty bird. Pretty bird. Pretty bird. Pretty bird. Pretty bird.
Pretty bird. Pretty bird. Pretty bird. Pretty bird. Pretty bird.
Pretty bird. Pretty bird. Pretty bird. Pretty bird. Pretty bird.
Pretty bird. Pretty bird. Pretty bird. Pretty bird. Pretty bird.
Pretty bird. Pretty bird. Pretty bird. Pretty bird. Pretty bird.
Pretty bird. Pretty bird. Pretty bird. Pretty bird. Pretty bird.
Pretty bird. Pretty bird. Pretty bird. Pretty bird. Pretty bird.
Pretty bird. Pretty bird. Pretty bird. Pretty bird. Pretty bird.

Poor Blinkie never picked up talking most likely because he was not a parrot. Parrots are smarter and have better mouth muscles. Meanwhile, the little girl played the record so many times and with such fervor it began to skip and skip and then, one day, it mysteriously disappeared.

Just like Blinkie.

When the little girl left for school one morning, Blinkie was there. When she came home from school in the afternoon, Blinkie was gone. His cage was on the front porch and the drunk bastard mother said with a confused but semihappy look on her face, *I went to change his water and he must have snuck out and flew away.* Oh well. Too bad so sad. We can get another parakeet. It was strange that the mother put the cage outside in the first place. Strange that the water needed changing, as the little girl always kept it fresh. Strange that Blinkie would have jumped through the water slot which was a space barely big enough for him to squeeze through. All of it was strange but when your mother tells you a story and you are a little girl those end up being the facts. Also in the fact pile is the fact that the little girl never trimmed Blinkie's wings because she wanted him to feel very alive even though he lived in a dining room and not the jungle. Now he was alive and gone.

The little girl went into action. First, she spread a white sheet out over the front lawn. Then she sprinkled birdseed all over the sheet. Then she put on her jelly shoes and circled the neighborhood block by block, scanning trees and roofs for blue movement until it became too dark for seeing small birds. Nothing. Not even one garbly goo. Her big feet were blistered from blanketing the neighborhood in bad footwear so she went home, sat in the living room recliner, and used an entire box of Kleenex to mop up the wet mess that poured out of her little girl face. This was the saddest thing that had ever happened. Sadder than dinosaur bones not being believed. Sadder than rain.

Blinkie the finger lander. Blinkie the shoulder rider. Blinkie the bed-fellow. He was gone and would probably starve to death or get eaten by some damn golden retriever.

Back in the tree house, the little girl put Blinkie out of her mind and instead, refocused on the current sad bird story of her life. Since she was going to be in the tree house for a while with the dying hummingbird, she settled in, resting her head against the wall that wasn't there and stretching out her long legs slowly like melancholy. The weather, at least, was nice. It was doing what weather did and she felt relaxed by it. Air moved through the tree house in a soft, quiet way. The sun thoughtfully warmed little girls and creatures everywhere, whether recovering from major sewing injuries or simply dying. The hummingbird shut its tiny black eyes and stopped trying to fly somewhere for once.

Time painted slow shadows across the lawn. The sun or the earth moved a little, she could never remember which one did what. There are just so many things to understand and a person has to prioritize. The little girl couldn't take the hummingbird inside the house. Too risky. There was a springer spaniel named Sparky in the living room and a turtle with no name living in the bathroom. And she didn't want to leave the hummingbird alone in the tree house. What if it was confused by its surroundings? What if it died all alone? The little girl wondered what her favorite grandmother would say about all of this. Probably something that started with . . .

Oh, Honey.

And then she'd pause.

And then she'd say,

Well . . .

And then she'd look at the little girl.

And the little girl would look at her.

And then, at last, after the appropriate amount of pausing and thinking, the favorite grandmother would slide a plate of day-old muffins
or banana bread in front of the little girl and mention something
about letting go of things that are beyond our control. Things like
lost or dying birds, or forgotten birthdays, or scars that resembled
tattoos. She would not mention all the crazy shit that she herself had
let go of. Like when the little girl's mother discovered her father's
Cadillac parked at a motel in the middle of the day and knocked on
the door to find out why he was parked at a motel in the middle of
the day and the answer was that he was making a major mistake with
a woman he had met at the ski lodge. She would not mention any of
that. She would also certainly not mention Jesus or chores which was
another reason this grandmother was her favorite grandmother.

Feeling reassured by all this hypothetical grandmother advice, the
little girl picked up her cross-stitch scene of pretty, crooked flowers
and wondered if they might straighten toward the sun over time, like
real flowers. Wondered if maybe she should just let them be. Maybe
nothing at all was missing here and she should just get a grip. The
hummingbird turned in her hand and opened one tiny eye, surprising
her like a sinkhole. It was panting now and making small wheezing

noises. Picture an ant playing an ant-sized accordion. That was the small and woeful song of the dying hummingbird.

A sudden urge to be heroic overtook the little girl and she felt a crackling inside her chest like she had swallowed a sparkler. She wanted to save everything. To believe everything could be saved. But saving the hummingbird was out of the question, things were too far gone and she was no veterinarian. Just a little girl with a sewing injury who really really liked bread. All she had was what she had. And so, the little girl set the cross-stitching down in her lap, lifted the broken hummingbird with its lolling string of tongue close to her mouth and whispered, *What if we both just lay here and pretended we were mysterious?*

BEAT A DEAD

BEFORE THE CART

They have sixty-six chromosomes, two more than the average
horse. Stocky and slightly squat, their black manes stand erect in
buzzed mohawks, defying gravity. A faint stripe runs down their
short legs, a telltale sign of primitive genes. Ranging in color from
sandy yellow to a dull tan, with longer hooves and thicker soles, these
are not the sexy, leggy horses of the wild, wild West. These are the
very old ones. The very first ones.

Before they were ever ridden, before they were ever milked, before
they were ever corralled or branded or spurred. Before they were
bred or hunted or saddled. Before whipped. Before broke. Before
roped, boarded, shoed. Reined in. Auctioned off. Put to pasture. Put
to work. Put down. Before they were *put* anywhere, they existed only
for themselves on land that did not yet belong to anyone. There were
no lines drawn in sand, no maps painted on parchment paper. Terri-
tories were marked only in sprays of urine. They gathered in small

families, stallions and mares staying with their preferred partners for years on end. Offspring keeping close to parents and leaving to form their own herds when the time was right for leaving. They moved freely across the land, sleeping and rolling and running, mounting and kicking and biting, following the tried and ancient grazing patterns of those that came before.

Then, over 5,500 years ago, somewhere on the steppes of Central Asia, it was decided by a species with two legs that a species with four legs could make them even faster, and the first saddle was strapped onto the first horse's back. The corral was erected, the bit pushed in and two became one, but this was no marriage. This was a conquering.

CRAZY

Getting on is always the easy part. One hand on the horn, one foot in the stirrup, I swing my leg over and settle into the warm curve of leather. He is boulder still, taking on my weight dutifully like he was taught. *Good horse.* This sturdy car of legs. This magic carpet of muscled velvet. He opens his mouth, and the bit clanks in. He works his jaw back and forth, grinding molar against metal, giving in to this pinching ghost snack. *Gentle horse.* I am six months pregnant but decide it's fine. We won't go too fast. And besides, I want my baby to know the buoyant feeling of being carried by a horse. Maybe it will wake him up, ignite something wild in him. Or maybe I am just a pregnant girl tired of all the pregnant girl rules and for once I allow myself to do something crazy. Gray with flecks of white fire-cracking across his flank, he is ready to be steered, and we set off.

WITH NO NAME

Listen to this wild lesson. Most wild horses today are not actually wild. Not really and truly. The mustangs that frolic in Montana tourism commercials appear wild, but are actually descendants of domesticated horses. Stray cavalry ponies. Wayward ranch stock. Genetically diluted odd-toed ungulates. We took wild horses from the wild, tamed them and bred them so we could have them and ride them, then some of those horses hopped the fence and went back to running wild again. Though their manes fly in a tangled mess, their hooves paw at the ground un-shoed and stuffed with clumps of clay, don't let these fence hoppers fool you. Their pure, original wildness is gone forever. There is a way to prove it with needles and blood and tests. Degrees. Levels. Percentages of purity. Once something is owned it can no longer be wild. You can argue about wildness, go ahead. But it won't get you anywhere.

Now, instead of Mongolian, these horses are named feral. Feral means *having reverted to the wild state.* The Latin word for feral is *feralis.* Meaning *funerary.* Meaning *fatal.* Meaning *of the dead* or *fierce.* Meaning *ferocious.* Meaning *vicious.* Meaning *savage.* Meaning *predatory. Menacing. Bloodthirsty.*

WAR

We are racing now, and racing is not in my blood. How can a thing with legs be this fast? His body is crazed with speed, his long muscles spinning and wild and sweating underneath me. I clutch hard with both of my legs and put my head down instinctively, but I am no jockey. Just a girl with a friend who has two horses. I take his dark, coarse mane into my mouth, and I am surprised when it tastes like nothing, like ordinary hair. I crunch down on it with my teeth because I can. The tree is coming closer now, the only tree in the field. He will see the tree, he has to see the tree. His mouth is foaming like war, and he is so far gone. All I feel is wind. All he feels is home. I think of the helmet hanging on a rusty nail back at the barn. The helmet that would have flattened my freshly washed hair. I pull and pull on the reins but the bar of metal shoved into his mouth means nothing to him. How could I have mounted a thing this wild? We will die against this tree I think. Me, my baby, and this horse. We will all die being fast.

I cannot hear the screams of my friend. She sees us speeding toward the tree and tries to help, but her voice has disappeared into the rushing wind and clomping hooves. She is so beautiful, my friend. All blonde and sharp angles. She always lights a cigarette right after mounting her horse and takes a big sexy drag like she doesn't give a rip. I never ask her why she does that, and anyway it doesn't matter. I like watching her do it. She used to work on a horse farm in Montana where she dated this truck driver named Jeff. She always takes a big drag when she talks about Jeff. Now she lives in Minnesota and is married to a guy she knew from high school. Her husband adores her, but she gets really pissed when he holds her hand in public. He installs security systems. She says he is so boring and is obsessed with the missionary position. I don't like the way she talks about her husband, but I listen anyway because marriage is hard and these are her horses.

She recently took off her shirt for her neighbor while they were alone in his basement playing foosball. She thinks this might be the start of something. When she tells me I say, *Oh wow, oh really* and grip the reins a little tighter. I think she likes the feeling of shocking me, but I'm not all that shocked. When you stay inside a house all day with small children, it sometimes makes you want to do things like bang your head against the wall or bang your neighbor. This I can understand.

In Mongolia there exists a certain breed of horse that they say is still wild. That they say was never domesticated. In the late nineteenth century, a wildly determined Russian explorer and naturalist named Przewalski was on the hunt for these truly wild horses and he was presented with the skull and hide of a wild horse that had been shot near the Chinese-Russian border. Wild horse experts analyzed the dead skull and the dead hide of the dead wild horse and determined that, yes, this dead skull and dead hide belonged to a truly wild horse. Thankfully, the horse was now dead, so his wildness could be determined once and for all.

ALL THE PRETTY

Earlier that day, when we first met and things were calmer, I stroked the fine velvet of his nose and wondered if my fist would fit into one of his gaping nostrils. His overgrown black mane hung in strawlike clumps over one eye in a very teenager way. I held some grain in my hand and loved the feeling of his fat horse lips lapping at my upturned palm, his wiry chin stubble pushing against my fingers. Keep your hand flat and his teeth will not bite into you. One horse rule that everyone should know.

The trail weaves through open meadows of restored prairie grasses and underneath archways of massive bur oaks, their curvy leaves already transforming into fall's fiery copper. Minnesota dazzles this time of year, and this park reserve in Hanover pulses rich with color. The air is damp and cool, heavy with that distinct before-winter smell of decaying leaves. Garter snakes shoot across the trail as if from tiny cannons, their green tails disappearing covertly into silent grass; one final flick and they were never there. We get to the little lake and let our horses wade into the water up to the bottom of our saddles. She shows me how to lay my head all the way back so I am lying down on my horse's rump. All I can see now is a white mess of clouds and the rustling red and orange of late autumn. I don't tell my friend this, but I am secretly on board with the missionary position. I don't tell her that sometimes I ask my husband to lay on top of me for no reason. Like how some people cover themselves with a weighted blanket to get through a thunderstorm. All that heaviness making you calm, making you stay exactly where you are. Being just a little bit crushed, but still okay enough to breathe.

I can feel my horse getting restless underneath me in the water. I grip tighter with my thighs and dig my nails into my palms as hard as I can. It is almost over. It is always almost over. Knowing there are moments like this makes me ache and ache. Peace. Calm. The fresh air soothes me like a mother. I am a guest on this horse. This special occasion feels borrowed, and I want more. More horse, more little hidden lake, more mud caked on the bottom of my boots. More alive.

After the lake I will turn my horse around and head back to my suburban house. Back to my raised breakfast bar. Back to my children. I will walk inside, sit on furniture that is bought and paid for, and notice it is time to vacuum once again. And that will all feel just fine. But out here, lying on this horse in this glistening lake, here I feel a primordial sense of home and calm, as if my body belongs here. As if I have finally made it back to where I began. Our horses snort and splash in the water. A single white crane lands soundlessly, and the lake haloes out from under her impossibly thin body. I look over at my very pretty friend and notice that her eyes are closed.

ALL THE KINGS

And after he has been gentled, where does he store his rage? I imagine at night he wakes suddenly, and rears up, pawing at the thick wooden boards of his stall, not knowing what he is after, knowing only that he wants out. Making a sound like trapped thunder.

OF COURSE, OF COURSE

Though wild Mongolian horses were hunted almost to extinction in the 1960s, a few survived in captivity and due to a successful breeding program they are making a comeback. A few small herds now graze the fields of Mongolian national parks where their social behaviors are, of course, continuously monitored to help with worldwide husbandry efforts. Researchers have learned that these horses gather in small families, stallions and mares staying with their preferred partners for years on end. That offspring keep close to parents and leave to form their own herds when the time is right for leaving. That they move freely across the land, sleeping and rolling and running, mounting and kicking and biting, following the tried and ancient grazing patterns of those that came before.

WHISPERER

After the little lake and right before we hit the tree at a full gallop, my horse swerves, and I surprise myself by hanging on. I yank the reins as hard as I can, and he slows to a stop. I let the thin straps of leather fall, swing my legs over his great, sweating back and sink into prairie grass, alive and shaking. My hands go to my belly, and I whisper to my unborn son that I am so very sorry. My ears ring with sudden stillness.

For the first time I hate horses.

My friend catches up with me and says, congratulations, I'm the most badass out of all her girlfriends. She likes to go fast, and she only likes to ride with people who like to go fast. If her horse isn't going fast enough she stops on the side of the trail, yanks a switch from a tree, and smacks him in the flank over and over. She says you have to show your horse that you mean business. If he tries to stop and munch on some weeds, don't let him do it, she says. He'll just get lazy and fat, and it's all downhill from there.

COULDN'T DRAG ME AWAY

The new population of wild Mongolian horses has recently been deemed genetically sustainable. There is a studbook somewhere in Prague, which details the exact percentage of wildness of every single one on planet Earth. In case you were wondering.

The last time I ever rode with my friend my horse got spooked by a snake and bucked me off. As he went up on his hind legs I rolled backward off him and landed hard on my back. My foot was caught in the stirrup, and he dragged me through the gravel for a few seconds before running into the woods. I called him a motherfucker and ran

22

after him, and my friend just sat there on her horse laughing. I caught up to my horse and got back on, but later that year my friend dug a deep hole in the ground and shot him up with barbiturates. He was old and anyway she didn't want her daughters riding an unpredictable horse like that. Horses are so heavy, you can't just drag them to their graves, she explained. It's easier if you just let them fall.

BEAUTIFUL WEATHERS

A COLLAGE ESSAY

It began with no ado.

Spring, Summer, Autumn, Winter

I did not know where the drift of
weather, or the iron tide of chance would take me.

I'm not jumping your shit.
I don't want you to think I'm jumping your shit.

At first I loved winter.
If snow is falling it's unutterably beautiful,
calm, and falling whitely.
Cold weather kept odors to a minimum.
The wind shows us how close to the edge we are.
And I have a really good feeling about this Christmas.

And then one night it snowed.

And then snowed some more.

And then I wake to how winter it is.

I've got to buy some proper winter boots. Winter clothes.

Shit in your hat, and then put it on your head.

I am trying to be realistic.

(You just be brave. You make that a policy. Just remember, what

doesn't kill you will make you stronger.)

Hold up winter, that shivering truth,

that season that refuses to bloom.

It is silent forever in this new world,

aggressively boring.

But it was a strange boredom;

one human simply missing other humans.

Winter, the weather of catastrophe, is hanging on.

God save our life.

Meek little wives feel the edge of the carving knife and study their
husbands' necks.

Indians would throw themselves into the sea when the bad wind
blew.

Only the thin river held a trickle of sun.

It doesn't matter.

I can scarcely wring a poor laugh out of this wretched body anymore.

I find that death is simple,
not like life at all.

We have all seen a sliver of light in the sky; we have all seen the cres-
cent moon by day.

The thing to do, we decided, was to forget the coffee and switch to
gin.

Nothing could happen until you stopped hoping for it.

These were the right thoughts.

It was early spring, before anything had bloomed, and the grass was
gray and mush and rotted.

The snows disappeared, our ears popped; the trees changed; and in
the trees were strange birds.

We're nothing if not persistent.

Then.

Like a window thrown open,
that unresistant green of a painted, slippery grass lets us leap as if
the earth is a trampoline, a paradise.

Spring exploded miraculously the way it always does.

Nothing we do will ever be as free as this;
so much green spilled into blue.

It is difficult to know when looking at something beautiful where the
beauty is actually coming from.

Deep into spring, when the sun shines, then go out into it.

But nobody wants to read about other people being happy.

So.

It was tough getting dates that summer.
Every booze party ends in a fight.

The warm air smelled of mildew and then a flood of summer rain.
Rain falling on a summer night is lovely.
At first it was pleasant, now there's no stopping it.

Since morning it's been raining.
Rain all day, the damp fungal scent.

All that summer long panels of transparent golden silk would blow
    out the windows and get tangled and drenched in the afternoon
    thunderstorms.

When the rain speaks then stay at its side and listen well.

This sky, those manes of wild light,
details from the August heat.

I am hungry for nothing.
It's the heat.
The fan flips the air around but doesn't make it any cooler.

It's the thickness of the air, the sun caught in the trees.

It was so hot the people never left their houses.

It was so hot men's balls hung down to their knees, and the men had
to tie them up.

It was so hot fish at the bottom of the river
burned like silk touched to a flame.

Bad smells, seasons changing—heat and cold,

the effects of alcohol and how it makes you say and do dumb things
and have dumb sex.

And then autumn.

And then cool night air.

I drove North.

I had no plan.

The land was mostly wilderness.

Was anyone ever so young?

And blackbirds do fly back to their roosts.

Their black wings tucked against the wind like men in coats.

When leaves turn in autumn, the burning flame of red sets the entire
face of the moon on fire.

How could I ever be unhappy with these colors in piles around me?
Beauty is precious because it is brief.

We had, it seems, loved the planet and loved our lives, but could no
    longer remember the way of them. Where do we all go wrong?

They make it seem natural to love what ends.

The moon was full and hanging low like a pregnant cat.
There were stars.
A lot of the stars were missing, but there were still too many to count.

I never finish the last sip of wine. It's too sad.

This is all I have to tell you.

There is a whole strange world underneath us where things are done differently. That startling moment where, once the goggles are properly adjusted, you can really see what's going on. Where all who swim become clear. The ones who exist in that constant state of float, that hug of wet air, that slow moonwalking dream.

And the zombie-faced puffers, the ghostly slick freaks, the Monet-bellied clowns, they become the real ones. Instead of walk, there is *flutter*. Instead of run, there is *dart*. Instead of jump, there is *breach*. Also, *alongside* means something else.

Imagine.

Imagine he is pregnant.

Imagine he is pregnant and his smooth, flat stomach is swelling.

Imagine he is pregnant and his smooth, flat stomach is swelling and imagine him waking just before dawn. He is standing in his front doorway, bathing in new sunlight, and his wife comes up behind him. She is lovely and long, like him, ethereal almost. She has curves like no other. This pair could be mistaken for twins. She moves in a slow circle around him, appreciating all his body is doing for her, for them. She wraps one leg around him, runs that leg slowly up and down his bulging body, and presses her forehead lovingly to his. After their eyes lock, after they've said, *I see you, and I know you* without opening their mouths, after this predawn dance, she then floats off to work, leaving him to putter around the house all day.

Until I started staying home, I never realized how many nicks there were in the walls. Especially in the living room where the kids play. White flaking out from under all that Sea Foam Blue. Gouges, really. My husband tells me we should just repaint the whole thing. But who has time for that? So I take a Q-tip, blob the white spots back to blue and there you have it. My living room is back in order.

While she is gone he eats and waits. He sucks food into his mouth almost like a vacuum. While eating and waiting, he hangs on to the furniture as if his life depended on it, as if he might be carried away by the slightest breeze. As if he never quite learned how to stay.

After many days of eating and dancing slow and resting, when he has more than doubled in size, things will begin to happen. His bulging body will begin throbbing subtly at first, it will feel like cramps or a dull backache, but soon enough contractions will rip through his skeleton (yes, he has one) and consume him. He will writhe in pain. He will wrap his leg around something tall and straight, think of a floor lamp or a cat scratching post, and he will cling to that as he pushes. Finally, after some time, after he thinks he can no longer handle the pain, he will open up all the way and one thousand tiny babies will explode quietly from his body like underwater fireworks.

One night after having enough, I dragged my two little boys from their beds and buckled them into their car seats. I sat in the garage gripping the steering wheel, holding on until my knuckles turned white. I didn't have anywhere to go, so I just started driving. After only thirty minutes, I turned the car around and headed home. When I got there, I curled my limbs around my husband's sleeping body to check for signs of life.

When this is done, when the pushing is all over and there is nothing left, his body will go limp, and he will fall, as if in slow motion, to the floor in exhaustion. He will lie there on that floor for a short time, maybe two minutes, maybe four, until his wife comes home and sees that it's all over. She won't wonder about the thousand tiny babies, she already knows they will be gone. She won't take any pictures. There will be no glass of water. She won't even shake her head slowly back and forth. She will react exactly as if exploding this much life into the world was normal. She will lie down next to him and gently nudge him until he is sitting up. He will not want to do this, but he will. He will sit up because now is the right time for sitting up.

It is the middle of the night and I am in my bed. One has a fever of one hundred and three. The other has the croup, his ragged breath wheezing out from between his bluish lips. It sounds like air being torn.

And I am alone.

And no one is with me.

And somewhere, I later learn, a phone has gone dead in a bar.

And because they only have up to five years, and because only one out of their one thousand tiny babies will even survive, and because they could be plucked out of their home at any moment, their small still-breathing bodies dumped onto concrete and left to suffocate, crack and dry in the sun, because their dead, shriveled flesh retails for as much as three thousand dollars per kilogram, because both of them could easily be lost in storm-roiled seas, and because many before them, *most* before them, have been ground up and ingested by others who wish to bear life but cannot, for all of these reasons she will not waste any time. She will wrap one leg around him and slip herself into his empty body, filling him with one thousand new eggs.

———————

From the other side of the bedroom he says that he is sorry, the softness of his voice an unexpected weight, like flowers laid gently on my chest. We have both fallen in small ways. I put down my book and crack right open, clumsy and wet and ready for another round.

———————

Under the cover of water, nestled between whispering blades of seagrass, together, the two seahorses let go of their anchors and drift upward nose-to-nose, spiraling slowly as they rise. And they begin again.

———————

My foot reached for your foot in the middle of the night, and you quickly kicked it away. You don't like to be bothered while you sleep. I need to understand this.

When I was six or seven, I dug a deep hole into the snowdrift in my grandma's front yard. Bundled up in a too-small navy snowsuit that pinched my crotch, I was out there alone, and that's the way I liked it. I could make up stories. I could say swear words. *Shit, shit, shit,* I chanted as I dug, daring one of the adults inside to hear me. I dug and dug with small mittened hands. I dug from the top down, two-handed, flinging the snow behind me like a dog in the sand. I dug because I was weird and my sisters hated me and the sun was out. I dug because I had nothing else to do on a Sunday in February but disappear into a silent, white hole. I dug because I loved the cold and the way I could survive in it already. So skinny my doctor thought I was anemic, yet so fierce, I could withstand winter's harsh slap across my face for hours and hours. On ice skates. On skis. On anything.

Cheeks numb. Snot frozen in streaks across my mittens. Eyelashes snowflaked and clumped. I felt at home in the cold and snow, prancing through frozen turf like a two-legged reindeer, learning early on to love the way winter cleaned and covered and silenced the world. Learning early on to love its icy grip.

I dug and dug until I hit bottom and then I fell into the hole headfirst. This was a surprise, but it immediately made sense. The hole was too straight down. I should have come at it from the side, more of an angle. I remember a quiet thud and then stillness. Nothing. With my arms pinned to my sides, and my face pressed against frozen ground, there was nothing I could do. It was quiet. I was upside down, my pink moon boots sticking out of the snow above me. I should have panicked but I didn't. I felt calm, like I was in a kind of secret hug.

In the past two weeks, school has been canceled five times. It has been very cold. There has been a lot of snow. My chickens' eggs crack and freeze the moment they hit the ground. Ice dams threaten our roof. It's another February in Minnesota and much of the Midwest is colder than the Northern arctic, some cities reaching temperatures of fifty below. Seventeen people have died. Cities have declared snow emergencies, and no one can park in the streets. After each school closing announcement, my two boys bounce around the house screaming in ecstasy like they won a box of fucking puppies, and I can't get any work done. Laundry piles up. I have to wear the small underwear, and they cut into me, leaving angry red lines behind.

I sit at my computer editing dialogue an hour before dress rehearsal, and I hear my oldest son say to his brother, *She's probably just on*

Facebook. He's mad because I won't play cribbage with him. I'm mad because I can't just play cribbage with him. My new play opens in three days, and there is still so much work to do. My husband is directing the play, and since it's tech week, he is always at the theater. *Our* theater. A small theater in a small suburb of Minneapolis that we founded together twelve years ago. A passion project that we began on a whim after having a baby in New York and immediately deciding to come home. At first it was exciting. Now it pays the bills. I look out my kitchen window and the snow falls and falls, blanketing my street flake by white flake, burying the cars and the trees and the fire hydrants, forcing small birds to huddle inside the pine trees. Piles and piles of heavy wonderland for all of us to move through.

I have twenty-five minutes to get dinner into the three of us, pick up the sitter, and get to rehearsal and I receive an automated call from the school district saying due to the extreme cold, school will be closed for the next three days. I crack store-bought eggs into a pan on the stove and push them around with a wooden spoon.
Eggs again.

This is not a normal winter. We haven't seen cold and snow like this since the '90s. One night, after staying up late watching a dumb romantic comedy, I find myself on the toilet crying uncontrollably, a wad of soggy toilet paper in my lap. Sobs coming in waves, my ribs

aching, I just can't get my shit together. Maybe it's the cold and end-
less snow. My husband and I haven't touched each other in weeks.
The news cycle has been sickening. Hundreds of families seeking
asylum at the border and children being ripped from the arms of their
parents. I use the last of the toilet paper and reach for a hand towel.
I tell myself not to crumble, but I crumble anyway. Our house is very
small and the bathroom is really the only place to bawl your face off.

When you get to this phase in your crying there's no untangling anything. It exists in one big rolled-up yarn ball of pain under your rib
cage and feels very hot like a sock full of rice that's been in the mi-
crowave. Your dog slumps against the bathroom door, wondering
what's going on in there. You see the shadow of him under the door
and know that his big fluffy dog body is pressed against the wood as
hard as it will go. This bathroom scene is upsetting him and he's not
going anywhere. That's his girl in there.

A dead humpback whale is discovered in the Amazon rainforest. Apparently it is unusual for a humpback whale to be anywhere near the
northern coast of Brazil in February. Very rarely do humpback
whales travel that far north. Sea levels have been rising and rough
winds may have flung the whale to the swampy mangroves where it
was found. The whale, an adolescent, is estimated to weigh 10 tons.

There is no way to remove the body because officials cannot get a bulldozer across the swamp to remove the carcass. In the video, a man and a woman in tan windbreakers and hiking boots are walking around the dead whale. They have clipboards and speak in loud whispers, as if they are afraid of waking the whale up from his nap. They think it may be a calf who was separated from his mother during migration. They are planning to let the carcass decompose and then they will dismantle and display the skeleton in a natural history museum. A whale in the rainforest seems like an important discovery, but I suppose anything being in a strange place seems important. A polar bear wandering inland. A snowy owl nesting in California. A little girl in her grandmother's yard, upside down in a hole of snow. All of us suddenly thrust into places where we don't belong.

I find it just a little bit sad that even though a whale can sing and give birth and travel thousands of miles and maybe even love, we decide its being dead in the forest is the thing that makes it strange. Already. Already we have moved past the singing.

The next-door neighbor had warned us about ice dams. Hanging in front of our living room window is a row of freakishly long, sinister icicles. Deathly sharp, they jut medieval-like from the roof, like the fangs of a very toothy, very abominable monster, threatening to pierce our snow-piled window boxes at any moment. They are so large, so very attached to the gutters, that whacking at them with a shovel would be too dangerous. We don't have one of those long rakes to shovel the snow off the roof. We also don't have a snow blower. We could buy two plane tickets to somewhere warm, or we could buy a long rake and a snow blower, and while that argument seems valid enough, we don't ever actually buy two plane tickets to go anywhere warm.

I Google *ice dams* and read that they are caused by a complex interaction between heat loss from a house, snow cover, and outside temperature. For dams to form, there must be snow on the roof, some parts of the roof have to be above 32 degrees and other parts of the roof have to be below 32 degrees. The dam grows as it's fed melting water above it. The water above it will get backed up and find cracks and openings and seep inside and make your ceilings into wet cardboard, and if that happens on a Monday, it will feel extra worse because you have already sworn off drinking wine on Mondays and now your ceilings are soggy and yellow and cracked and you have nothing left to live for. I read something about *conduction, convection,* and *radiation,* but I lose focus during that part of the article because the cat has the hiccups, and it's kind of hilarious.

My husband sends me to the gas station a block away for ice melt. I have to ask what ice melt is. *Salt,* he says. Oh. We have never bought salt before. It's bad for the dog's paws and for the environment in general. But now we have to buy salt and put it on our roof and hurt the dog and kill the environment because we have to save our old little house from being swallowed by ice and the neighbors are beginning to talk. I'm not sure if dumping a large bag of salt on our roof is going to help. I'm pretty sure most of it will just slide off and end up on our flower boxes and also destroy any chance of the flowers coming up in the spring, but that's what the bearded experts on YouTube say so that's what we do.

If it hadn't been for the birds circling overhead, no one would have known about the whale. He would have just laid there, decomposing on his own, free from experts and their windbreakers, their assessments. The thought occurs to me that he could have been alive when the giant wave brought him there. No one knows, of course, but it's possible. I wonder how long it would take for a whale to die on land. A quick online search tells me not very long. A few minutes, maybe. A whale on land is very quickly crushed by its own weight because a whale weighs thousands of pounds and land is a nonbuoyant environment. I think that land being a nonbuoyant environment is fairly obvious, but maybe some people just don't realize. I wonder if a whale can even sing on land.

I want him to be able to. .

I am sitting at my kitchen table writing, and I see a truck pull up across the street. Two men wearing bright yellow jackets and pants drag red hoses from their truck to the front of the neighbor's house. They circle the house for fifteen minutes, looking up, assessing the situation. One pulls a ladder from the truck bed, hoists it up onto his shoulders, and drags it through the snowdrift in the front yard, setting it up against the roof. He climbs to the top and begins attacking the outside of the little yellow house with steam that shoots from the end of his hose. Icicles the size of human thighs crash into the snow dramatically. As the men work, the whole house disappears inside a bomb of steam. They melt and chisel and beat the ice back. It is well below zero. They are very serious with their hoses, like firefighters, but this occasion doesn't feel urgent like fire. The ice has moved slowly and politely, building up drop by drop in accordance with the level of precipitation and temperature fluctuation over the course of weeks and weeks. But suddenly, the ice has been deemed extremely dangerous. Suddenly, it has got to go.

After watching the men work for a while I have to turn away. I don't like the way they're beating the ice down with their hoses, fighting water with more water. Turning water against itself like that.

All the blood is rushing to my head. It is very quiet, and I am breathing fine. I see stars. There is a sense of solemn wonder down here. A sense of me and only me. I imagine this is what it feels like in the womb, serene and silent and cross-armed. Whether I am being gently cradled or slowly crushed, I do not know. Winter has begun to claim my small, skinny body, and I don't even mind. It doesn't feel wrong.

I wonder if he felt scared, all alone and under trees like that. Did he marvel at the soft wind on his skin, the sudden absence of water, the green leaves that floated down from the sky to settle around his body? What does it feel like to be crushed by your own weight? To be claimed by dry air? To learn for the first time you weigh anything at all?

I hear my own voice say to my own son, *Please, please just let Mom work.* He is almost twelve. He is curled up next to me on the bed, his eyes on my screen, one hand petting the dog. The temperature outside is at minus 30 degrees, and the walls have closed in on us, making our two-bedroom bungalow feel even smaller. The chickens have begun eating their own eggs. A ninety-year-old woman was found dead outside of her house in Michigan, having accidentally locked herself out while feeding the birds. *Please, please let Mom work. Just for fifteen minutes. Just a little bit.* I am behind. Now that my play has opened I am catching up on other work. Readings for grad school. Essays that need revision. Grants for my theater. I am tired, and my patience has waned. My son stiffens. Uncurls himself. Walks to the bedroom door. I hear myself say I'm sorry. Ask if he's upset. His hand turns the knob, and the truth is that I want him here, but I just can't have both. There is one tiny blackhead on his nose. He is becoming a man, and I am finally becoming something other than mother. Sometimes I want to go backward to a time when all I did was play with him and be with him, before I felt the need to achieve more than that. Balancing it all feels like madness. I sometimes imagine what it would be like to be alone, without a husband, without children, how much easier things would be. But my love for them is its own kind of madness; it centers and strengthens even as it whips and pulls.

He leaves my bedroom. I turn to my screen and read a sentence about whales. An essay has recently been accepted into a book that sounds important, and I try to write faster, but the door keeps opening. Snack inquiries. Has the cat been fed? What time am I leaving for the theater tonight? Math homework. I remember I have already written an essay about whales. I tell myself I need to diversify. Write more about land animals. Something slower and less majestic. Birds that don't fly come to mind. Or tortoises.

Everyone is getting bloody noses. The air inside our house is dry, and I can't keep enough lotion on my hands. I tug a freshly washed mattress cover onto my son's bed, and the static shocks me into screaming, *Motherfucker!* A huge spark explodes from the blanket, like some kind of Harry Potter magic wand shit, zapping me on the end of my index finger where I had picked the skin away after reading the bad reviews of my play. I hadn't even noticed the skin was gone until I shocked myself.

The snow continues to fall, and I obsess about the dog's paws and keeping the birdfeeder full. The temperature dips even lower, and my boys haul our four chickens inside, stuffing them into the dog kennel in the basement—a complicated task that involves sequestering the dog and cat, erecting a roosting perch, and covering the kennel floor with brown paper bags. In the morning, the smell almost knocks me over. Spilled water mixed with shit mixed with chicken feed oozing over the sides of the kennel floor. After cleaning up the mess and hauling the birds back outside, I vow never to bring them in again, but the next day it's even colder, and my boys plead with real tears to bring the chickens back inside. This time I don't feed or water them, so they're nice and warm, but now they're starving and dehydrated. It doesn't even matter because they shit all over the place anyway and I have to clean it all up again.

On my way home from the theater, I see two wild turkeys huddled under a small awning in front of a learning center called Tinker Thinkers down the block from our house. I stop the car and roll down my window. I've never seen wild turkeys on Main Street before. The turkeys stand on one leg pecking at the glass desperately like they need to get in there and learn some stuff. I've thought about checking the place out. I can't even help my youngest son with this thing called a number line that involves Friendly numbers. Apparently, numbers ending in zero or five are Friendly because they are easier. I want to ask my son if the other numbers are called Assholes, but I don't ask him that because he's nine. *You guys okay?* I shout out my window at the shivering turkeys. They don't answer me. The awning is keeping them out of the snow, and my basement is already full of birds that shouldn't be there, so I drive away.

At the bus stop, a short woman with very small feet is standing next to me. We are both waiting for our children. She wears black-and-tan Sorel boots that are so small they look like they belong to a doll. As I stare at her very small, very unrealistic feet my dog pushes his nose into her crotch, and I have to apologize. I grab my son's hand, and we head home. Navigating the sidewalks has become treacherous, and we trudge through narrow tunnels of snow with our heads down like bundled-up voles. The snowbanks tower over the top of my son's head and in some places over the top of my head. I worry a car might hit him as he emerges from a tunnel on the corner of the street. I hold his mittened hand in my mittened hand, and we do not talk because scarves cover our mouths and most of his questions are about snacks and basketball anyway so they can wait. We climb over a giant barrier of snow that one neighbor neglected to shovel, arriving safely on the other side together. My dog pulls and pulls on his leash, knowing he is about to be fed.

I try to put the dead whale story behind me, but then I have a dream that he is not fully dead and someone needs to push him back into the water. I'm trying to find the experts in the tan windbreakers, but they aren't there. I push and push on the whale, worried I will hurt him, but it's no use. The whale will not be moved.

I sit up in bed and wonder if I should go to the bathroom or eat a bowl of cereal. Then I wonder about the adolescent whale's mother. If she knew where her baby was, would she try to make her way from the ocean's edge into the forest? Wait at the mouth of the Amazon River until the ocean became angry enough again, large enough again, to pick her up and fling another whale, a mother this time, past the swamp and into the thick mangroves? Would she defy her own migratory pattern and travel too far north? In the pictures, the whale looks ghostly and beautiful lying underneath the green trees; peaceful and completely intact, with no visible injuries. He is just there, as if he had always grown there among those gnarled trees. A still and silent ocean dweller at rest under the leaves. Trees and whales and the things that water can do. A mother singing or not singing. Crying or not crying. Torn maybe, between where she wants to be, and where she knows she needs to go.

I lean back into my pillow, knowing I won't be able to fall back to sleep. The dog snores softly. I wait for morning and another snow day with my boys.

I'm not 100 percent convinced it's the winter that is making me cry so hard on the toilet. That never-ending season that punishes even as you cheerfully embrace it with cross-country skis and a sauna in the basement. A son named Winter. Reverence for the cold, silent sky and the one hundred thousand million stars that burn up there like stunted fireworks. I have always loved the winter, even when it pushes into me like this. Walking from the garage to the house with a load of groceries, I sometimes remind myself to stop on the sidewalk and look up. I only let myself do this for a little while because if I stay out there too long in the cold looking up at something that beautiful I will probably freeze to the sidewalk or disappear.

I see another neighbor down the street unwrap an Amazon package on his porch. He produces a rake and begins pulling out the long handle section by section. When that's all done, he holds it clumsily in his hands and looks up at his roof. His ice dams are the only ones that are as big as ours, and now he's going to get rid of them. I wish he wouldn't because I was beginning to think that we were in this thing together.

Water starts seeping in from the seam in the living room window while I soak in the bathtub. My boys watch as a blue plastic cup fills drop by drop. It becomes a game to see how many more drops can fall before water splashes over the edge. One of them shoves the overflowing cup through the shower curtain to show me. I jump out of the tub, throw on my robe, my boots, my winter jacket and dive out into the cold with no plan whatsoever.

I know something needs to be done about the water leaking in, but all I can do is stand there in the deep snow staring up at the icicles while my hair hardens into frozen clumps of straw.

I remember as a little girl, letting winter have its way like this. The cold hardening me, turning parts of me to crystal, and me daring it to finish. My face and toes and fingers tingling with pain, warning me to go inside or else. Withstanding its harshness meant that I belonged out there, that I was chosen in some small way. Back then, back in that hole in the snow, I sensed a tenderness in winter's strong grip. Caught inside her blustering, frigid web, I was stunned but unharmed.

My boys see me standing motionless in the deep snow and frantically tap on the window. I can't hear them, but I know they are telling me to come inside. And so I do.

It is Monday night, my night off from the theater, which means I get to drink wine. We are all at the table for a rare family dinner of pork chops and roasted beets when my husband mentions that the kitchen ceiling is dripping. I look up and see yellow cracks spider-webbing above me, small bubbles appearing like magic in the paint. I don't have to get up on a chair and feel the ceiling to know that it is wet. Our neighbor was right. I take a sip of wine and finish eating my beets. I should be upset by water coming in through the roof, but I am not. I should jump out of my chair and start swearing my face off, but I don't. I stay there at the kitchen table with my family talking about basketball and not looking at the ceiling.

To live in a place where the air could kill you in a matter of minutes. A place where you have to constantly beat back the ice and water and snow with machines and hoses and shovels. A place that swallows and stills you. Engulfs and entombs you.

To have fallen in love with a season that kills. To not be able to help it. Even the wild birds have no business here.

I decide to let the cracks spread. I look up and decide they might be beautiful. Meandering and fine as hairs, small yellow rivers spreading silently above my little family, bubbling and animating our Monday night dinner scene. Fine. I have spent my entire adult life trying to keep things warm and dry and smooth and clean, beating back danger, balancing it all. Trying to keep the cracks from spreading, the water from seeping, the cold from entering. Fighting against elements that I know deep down will, in the end, win anyway.

There is a strange kind of joy that happens when you allow something to become just a little bit ruined.

We finish dinner, and my husband borrows the neighbor's ladder, trudging it through the snow to the side of the house where the water is coming from. He leans it against the roof directly outside the window of my tiny office where I am trying to write. I hear banging, and the subsequent *clink, clink, clink* of ice chunks careening down. He bangs something sharp and heavy against the ice dams, over and over and over, shaking the whole house and upsetting the dog who is squashed against the door to my office, whining. I open the door, and he crashes in, sliding across the hardwood floor on his overgrown nails. My boys are fighting because one is in the bathtub and the other one needs to pee. I try to write, but there's too much noise. The sky begins to darken, but the pounding continues as my husband keeps going at the roof, beating back the thick shelves of ice with a hammer or a spade or some other kind of tool, trying to stop more water from leaking into the house.

Wildlife experts have noted that animals sometimes end up in places where they shouldn't be simply because they are curious. Yes, strange migration patterns are usually attributed to climate change, loss of habitat, and human interference, but some animals are just plain curious. Some animals purposefully veer off course because they are weird, because they want to see what else is out there.

I like this theory.

And then I feel myself being yanked out of the snow. Dangling upside down by my pink moon boots. My uncle's strong hands. Sudden brightness. Frost dusting his moustache. A gasp of frozen air hits my lungs. Gently, he sets me on the sidewalk. I stare up at him and he laughs a big laugh before heading into my grandma's house for egg bake. Dazed, I take a deep breath and check in with the sky. The winter birds are singing. The sun is out. I am alive. It is only after I am rescued from my hole in the snow that I understand I had been in trouble and begin to cry. I could have suffocated or been crushed by my own weight. I could have frozen to death all alone out there. It was lucky my uncle found me when he did.

But still. I miss that heavy thud of quiet. That dark white room of snow.

DEAR G.B.,

You're here again, and this time you're sitting on the sofa with my mom. I can't stop staring at your claws. Soft brown eyes like a middle school boyfriend and a nose as big as a coffee mug. Wet with snot. Slick, black lips. These details are almost too much, like a cartoon that I can smell. You pant hot, deep tuba breaths through your open mouth in perfect staccato rhythm. (Have you swallowed a metronome? Are we at band practice?) You're staring at me staring at you from across the living room entryway, one hand on the doorknob in case I need to escape. No offense.

This living room scene is appearing very dignified, and I fully expect finger sandwiches to be served on a wheelie cart any moment until my mom reaches out to pat your husky, unfamiliar shoulder like you're a visiting uncle from Indiana or something. I warn her not to do it, but she does it anyway. Even in dreams she refuses to listen to me. Her pointer finger is gnarled up from overuse or early arthritis or heavy drinking, we're not sure, but there's a big witchy knob growing right in the middle of it. She doesn't say but I know she's thinking your shoulder hair is coarser than it appears. Less like fur, more like small brown wires, probably useful for quick drying. How do you stand on the edge of a waterfall without falling in? Never mind. I say stupid boring things when I'm trying to get someone to like me.

My mom is too close, but because you are so beautiful maybe she thinks it doesn't matter. Maybe she thinks your beauty is a barrier, that you will always be this cool. But the moment she touches you with that knobby finger, you attack, swiping at her chest, her neck, her face with your black claws, each one of them a poised dagger. You are up on all fours on the sofa, cowering over her small body, a furry brown building ready for the kill. Your roar deafening. Your meaning precise.

My mom's last words are a gurgle.

Nice touch. Anyway, I thought you were in the bushes a few weeks ago, but it was just a giant bull moose eating leaves. His rack was exactly the size of a kitchen table and soaked in fuzzy velvet. He reminded me of Elton John. I stood there on a trail watching Elton John grunt and eat leaves with my family and some other families. It felt like we were watching TV, but it was real life, you know? Really happening. I took a lot of pictures though I was disappointed he wasn't you. Like the time I was trying to meet Sting after a concert by hanging around out back behind the dumpsters and all I met was his sister-in-law. I was nineteen and living in London, wearing a long velvet skirt that Elton John would have gone nuts over. My plan was to start singing the moment Sting emerged from the backstage door, and he would be overcome and invite me on tour. When instead I was shooed away from the dumpsters by the security guard, I went crying back to my Swiss Cottage flat, and on the way, I let a middle-aged guy with a greasy ponytail usher me into his closed café. He could have killed me but instead he made me a steak while I sat at the empty bar nursing my shattered dreams and feeling very sorry for myself that I wasn't on tour in the arms of my beloved.

You have the same initials as my favorite grandma, who is ninety-two. She slept on my couch just last week, and I took a picture of her sleeping because she looked so dead it was funny. She was wearing a white nightgown that was basically a doily with arm holes. Three squishy pink curlers nestled into her coifed hair, and her face wrinkles all piled off to one side like they were taking their own separate nap. All of her wags and swings. My grandma likes to be extremely naked in her kitchen extremely early in the morning. She says it's good to give yourself some air first thing. She misses VHS, and I tell her so do I. We drink wine and play Kings in the Corner until the cows come home. She tells me secrets about her marriage to my grandpa who once threw a frozen turkey at her head. How when he got sick he became much nicer because he couldn't drink anymore. How she was very grateful for those sick years.

My husband's grandma died just last night. We visited her in the hospital, and I could tell she was on her way out. It was cold in that hospital room, and her bare legs just laid there on top of the mattress, all skin and vein and bone. I would have covered them for her, but we didn't have that kind of a relationship. She had purple eyebrows tattooed onto her face, which probably saved her a lot of time in the long run. We had a hard time keeping that final conversation going because she was so weak. At her funeral people talked about how she folded fitted sheets very well. How she liked to complain to department store managers. How clean she kept her house. She liked things straight and tidy, but the mess of death came at her like a storm, breaking her bones, crunching her forward, squeezing her heart, until she was cold and gone and in the ground. I wonder how long her purple eyebrows will last down there.

I don't like to think about dying. About my body, this lanky cave of warm tissue that houses me, being gone. It's hard to not feel extremely important, like the world really needs me in it for balance. And for singing.

One park ranger in Canada told me a story about the time you ate a black bear just because. They deemed you dangerous and shot you three times, but you survived because you're so freaking enormous bullets just sink into your fat and evaporate like compost. You're still out there in the wild shredding things and scaring the adults. They call you The Boss. Maybe one day you will get sick and become nicer.

I'm worried I brought it on. The dream. The Great Mom Mauling. How you think things when you're sad or hurt or raging. And how those things burrow into your brain and manifest like crazed gremlins if you get them wet or feed them after midnight. She used to play the piano late at night while the rest of us were sleeping. I was too young to know what she was playing, but old enough to understand that it was beautiful. The air vent in my room went directly into the downstairs den where she played, so I pretended she was performing a private concert just for me. She played from memory, leaning into the foot pedal softly softly softly and then *WHAM* hard like she had a lover down there. I sometimes picture her on the other end of my air vent, eyes closed, fingers straight, pounding away at the keys after a long night of waitressing. It is comforting to know something else used to fill her up at night like that.

I love her, but she drinks so much her brain is falling apart. I love her, but I want to squeeze her face between my hands and shout into her face so loud that spit flies out.

It can be helpful to get away. See the sights. Have you ever been to New York City? I used to live there by a big cemetery with a lot of feral cats. I used to think, *I'm really doing it. I'm really doing the thing I said I was going to do.* Rain was exciting! Buying milk was exciting! I went there to sing on Broadway, but I didn't really do anything except eat a lot of chicken wings, get pregnant, and star in a Carpet King commercial. Agents gave it to me straight: Colgate commercials were definitely out. Okay, thank you for your time, motherfuckers. New York is like that. One minute it's killing you, and the next minute it's making love to you slowly in all the right places.

I miss the smell. It's like fresh waffle cones and forgotten-about chicken. Putrid and sweet like everything is alive and blooming and dead and rotting all at the same time. A real slam jam joy ride. Bodies oozing and flopping and careening right into you. Piles of garbage and then *BAM* Lindsey Lohan in a pantsuit. I bet you'd love it. Do you love anything, G.B.? I saw two of you making love once. Very far away, just two dots on a hill, but I zeroed in with binoculars, and then I saw that you were humping. At first it was exciting, but then I got bored, like how I feel when I watch the Super Bowl. It went on for so very long it got me wondering if maybe you couldn't finish? (It happens. Carry on cheerfully the next morning. Toast a bagel.) While you were draped over her like a Volkswagen she was poking around in the grass, turning over small rocks looking for grubs, wanting a snack break, but you kept at her. At one point you bit her neck roughly, forcing her back into position. I cringed when I saw that. I mean, it's easier to just imagine the bad things happening. And by easier I mean safer. And by safer I mean easier. And by easier I mean I don't know if people actually love me or if they are just tricking me.

My therapist says I'm wounded. You're supposed to take great care with wounded people because they are fragile, but wounded people can be very self-centered because they are always focused on their own big, goopy wounds. This one time my guts were hanging outside of my body dripping all over the kitchen floor. (This is a metaphor.) It was so unreal I couldn't believe it was happening. Eventually I put my guts back inside myself, but I think I put them back in the wrong order. So my spleen is where my diaphragm should be and my diaphragm is where my liver should be and my liver is where my small intestine should be and my small intestine is where my heart should be and my heart is where my appendix should be. At least it feels that way, I'm no organ specialist.

There are many ways to be ripped to shreds.

My class homecoming queen recently died of cervical cancer. The day she died, someone tagged me in a photo on Facebook that was taken the moment she was crowned. There I am, twenty years ago, standing behind her in a sparkly navy dress, my thin lips curled in disgust, my narrowed eyes boring hot holes into the back of her newly crowned head. Jealous. I wanted what she had. Straight hair, actual breasts, a blonde boyfriend who was good at singing. Now she is dead and buried in Colorado where there are a lot of sage bushes. After she died someone wrote on her brother's Facebook page that we should all vaccinate our daughters against HPV, and I wanted to rip that person's head off. What the actual fuck? People make me so angry I want to full-on throttle them sometimes. Just squeeze their throats a little bit to make them understand, you know what I mean? How dumb they are. How strong I am.

I'm trying to tell you everything I can think of.

Anyway. She was beautiful. The kind of beauty that is unfair, but you feel grateful that it exists. Her forehead was just the right size. When she smiled, her eyebrows stayed on the same plane. Her teeth were all perfectly lined up like geese. These are the right qualities for a homecoming queen to have.

You do this to me. Get me all riled up. When I see signs on the trail that say *Bear in Area* or *Bear Activity* or *You Are Entering Grizzly Country Get Ready to Be Ripped to Shreds You Dumb Idiots the Boss Is Probably Stalking You Right Now Bear Spray Is Useless You May as Well Spray Detangling Conditioner at an Oncoming Freight Train.* When I see signs like this my heart beats backward, and the back of my throat feels tinny like some loose change is stuck in there. Every pore in my body tingles, warning me to turn around. Go back. Danger.

I go deeper into the woods anyway because I have to. There are things in there I need to see. Air in there I need to breathe. You know what I'm talking about? All that green breathing in what we breathe out, turning it clean, handing it back to us and asking nothing in return like a very sneaky Secret Santa or the world's biggest golden retriever. Walking around in the woods I feel like for once I'm being properly held. No one is getting too hot, no one's arm is falling asleep. There's a real sense of stamina.

I dream about you, and you probably dream about licking ants. It's fine, I'm fine. Except I never wear the right colors when I'm hiking. The problem is that I like green so much that everything I buy is green. Green leggings, green shirt, green sports bra, green hat, green hiking boots, green rain jacket, green Nalgene. Other people exhibit some self-control, starting with a sensible base layer like gray or black and then building with a little pop of color from there. I start with green and then add more green. It's like a sickness the way I need green.

When I lived in Brooklyn I would walk through the cemetery just to look at the trees. I got in trouble by a security guard who accused me of exercising. After that I walked more slowly, meandering over to graves like I was visiting somebody. In my mind I imagined paying respects to Theodore Roosevelt's wife and Leonard Bernstein and Walter Hunt, who invented the safety pin. I stood at the graves long enough to make it look like I was conjuring up fond memories of picnics that we took together back when they were alive and healthy. I was such a liar.

I just remembered another homecoming queen friend of mine died. I drove to the cemetery and stood there imagining her pretty homecoming queen bones under that slab of concrete. It was the middle of winter, and the snow went all the way up to my thighs. I let it fill the tops of my boots, let it fall down into my socks and numb my calves. I still had skin that burned and flaked and freckled, turned hot and cold and clammy. The least I could do was stand there feeling something. We once went skinny-dipping in Lake Superior. It was freezing, and we screamed the entire time. She was the only girl I knew whose breasts were as small as mine, and I had loved her for it. We thought nothing could crush us. Not even huge waves from the hugest lake in the world. Not even little white pills. I felt sad standing there in the deep snow at her gravesite, and my tears left tiny frozen rivers on my face. There were no trees in that cemetery, which was fine. For once I was in a cemetery for the right reasons.

The homecoming queens are dropping like flies.

I've just gotten back into singing at funerals. It's not Broadway, but at least it's something. People show up expecting mediocrity, and I like to surprise them by blowing the roof off the place, really letting it rip. I can't stand when singers at funerals are bad. I mean people are dead up there. They mowed a lot of lawns/clocked in/found their G spots/skimmed the fat/fed the dogs/weather stripped/slow roasted/quick dried/got the pontoon back up and running/hurried home and then cancer or Alzheimer's ate their bodies, and they fought the good fight. They deserve Céline Dion. They deserve Beyoncé. I'm not trying to brag.

We dress up dead bodies and sing. You sit on dead bodies and wait. A teenage boy out for a run. A wilderness guide. Just this morning, a French composer out gathering nature sounds. Last year, a young mother and her ten-month-old. You were desperate. You had eaten a porcupine and the quills were slowly ripping your stomach/intestines/bowels to shreds, preventing you from putting on your winter weight. They say mother and baby died instantly, with the baby still strapped onto her mother's back. I saw a picture of them before it happened. The mother was outside, breathing in that green Canadian air, looking fresh and holy, her tiny blue-eyed baby peeking over her shoulder. I wonder if I'm supposed to feel sorry for you, but it's confusing.

In the dream I do nothing.

I just stand there in the doorway while you go at my mom, ripping bloody chunks from her body and shaking them between your teeth like a happy dog. I stand there watching, with more curiosity than horror, as you take apart my mother bit by bit. To you, she is no person. Just a piece of breathing meat, a passable source of protein. I know there's something going on here, some reason why this dream keeps coming back, and it's messing with me. I should dial 911 or chuck a pillow. *Something*. But I just stand there in the doorway like a hanging plant. Hooray. Daughter of the Year.

Once, I was hurt very badly by someone that I love. The pain made me think that I was dying. The pain made me wish that I was dying.

I could sometimes feel my heart tripping, it's rhythm off. *Good*, I thought. I spent a lot of time on the kitchen floor with my head leaning against the refrigerator because the refrigerator hummed reliably.

Heart pain is a killer.

I took pills for anxiety for a few months, but they made me not have orgasms, and I really like having orgasms, so no more pills for me. I'm on my own now. Worried and pill-less and ready for the sack. The pills took the edge off, but I missed living on the edge. Me and Aerosmith.

I can't stand this waiting. Let's get it over with already. A face-to-face encounter. A face-off. I figure if I can face you, if I can face a raging dewy-eyed boulder with jaws, then I can face the other things. The in-my-mind, middle-of-the-night things. The porcupine needles. Scenes on loop that rip right through your guts. I want them gone. I want to go out alone. I want my grizzly bear story, and I want it to be good.

We plan a family trip to Glacier. Bear spray arrives. I order books from the library to learn more about you on the sixteen-hour drive from Minnesota, but we leave before they arrive so instead I read a book by Miriam Toews. We pull in. It's glorious. June's first flowers quilt the hillsides in mighty pinks and reds and yellows. White bear grass blooming round and tall like furry sticks of cotton candy. Shaggy goats defying gravity, clinging effortlessly to slippery mountain faces, baa-ing like something straight out of *Sesame Street*. Elton John is there and munching away. Mountains, mountains,

mountains. It is Disney minus the rides, minus the everything made. I understand why you live here.

There are signs stapled everywhere. The trees, the fence posts, outside the bathrooms. Warnings. Updates. Instructions. Back away slowly. Play dead. Don't run. Don't climb. Don't move. Fight back. Belly down. Fingers laced. Protect your head. Grab a knife. Say a prayer. Your shit is everywhere on the trail, and it's probably fresh. I feel like punching my fist softly into the middle of it just to see if it reacts like bread dough. A friendly ranger in a wide-brimmed hat points out claw marks on a tree that start seven feet up and run all the way down. *Oof*, that was a big boy, she winks. Have a nice hike!

Day four and I am on the Swift Current Trail in East Glacier. It is late afternoon, and my husband has just left. He wanted to continue on, do a couple more miles, see the pretty lake, and so I need to hike back with the kids alone.

I panic. Change dispenses in the back of my throat. Bile builds. Heart beats backward. My boys. They are both still small and skinny, bare-lipped and bare-legged. All it would take is one quick swipe. I watch as my handsome husband disappears around a corner. Silence. I want to throw up.

I wasn't planning on taking the kids with me on my solo hike. I wanted it to just be a me-and-you thing. An uneventful meet-'n'-greet between fellow omnivores. Soulful yet safe. Artfully staged with maybe a couple of hummingbirds and a light mist. And if you decided to press my body into the dirt, crack open my rib cage and sink your teeth into my warm liver at least it would be just me. But no. Now I have to protect my offspring and all I have is one measly can of bear spray and some peanut butter Clif Bars.

The three of us hike. Holding hands and singing at the top of our squishy little lungs. "Edelweiss," "The Ants Go Marching," Lady Gaga, clumping along the trail as loud as we can. Fat marmots scatter, disappearing into impossibly small holes. Tiny brown squirrels cannonball from the brush at my feet, making me scream, making my boys scream, making us laugh at how easily we scream. When we're not looking down at our feet we are looking up at this glacier-carved heaven. Craggy mountain peaks dipped white with snow, lush valleys of spruce and cedar and alpine fir, and always, always a shimmering sapphire lake awaiting below. Around each corner lies majesty.

I hold my breath when the trail narrows, when I cannot see what lies ahead. Those blind curves. The overgrown brush. I brace myself, gripping the bear spray that knocks clumsily between my small breasts, bending my knees awkwardly in some sort of defensive ramble. My boys squish close behind, understanding that I must offer myself to you first, if it comes to that.

After an hour or so I feel better. Less attackable. The bile is gone. The sun is out. I've just received a compliment from a passing hiker on my green headscarf. My boys' voices give out but not mine, not yet. The ants go marching on and on and on and on and on. I know you are out there, a ghost in the bushes, but I allow myself to stop looking, at least for a little while. We finish our hike and head back to the campground. I make macaroni and cheese, and we eat it straight out of the pot. We see another moose, this time a mom with her calf, munching away on some leaves right there on the edge of the parking lot. We back away, giving her the space she needs. The sun is beginning to set, and we are all deliciously tired from our big adventure. Walking back to our campsite I feel small hands slip into mine and something aching and soft spreading slowly like warm honey under my ribs. An organ shifting back into place.

I go home with my neck a little sunburned. My feet a little blistered. My voice a little hoarse. My grizzly bear story isn't all that good. It lacked actual action. I basically just worked myself up over nothing. Lions and tigers and bears oh well.

Of course, two weeks after leaving Glacier, park rangers closed off the Swift Current Trail due to unusual grizzly bear activity. It's a shame we missed each other. Or not. I can't decide.

Another grandma has died. Another grandma down.

When I started writing you this letter my husband had two grandmas. Now he has no grandmas. She was one of the good ones. The banana bread and golf kind. The bingo kind. All smiles. She drove a red convertible and joked about finding a rich boyfriend with no moustache. This one died while singing at a birthday party. Death by song, can you imagine? Lying there in bed, her body looked deflated and done, like a late fall garden, finished and absent of its own glory. We are so very frail, all it takes is one small nudge and down we go.

And I cannot help but think.

That we will all end up in the ground with the earth piled up all around us. Whether or not we are beautiful. Whether or not we are kind. Whether or not we have taken Broadway by storm or remembered our daughters. Whether or not we are vicious or reckless or straight-toothed. Whether or not Sting has acknowledged our vocal potential. Whether or not our wounds have healed, if our displaced organs have settled back into place. If we have forgiven or been for-given. If we look good in a pantsuit or have loaded up on green. The earth's wet, mossy fingers will reach for us, and we will soften into soil. We will be eaten by the worms or by the birds or by the silent grass. Maybe by you, even. Nosing through a grassy meadow one day you'll heave over a large rock and there I'll be, eyeless and wriggling and flailing around in the sudden shock of sunlight, and you will pop me into your mouth like candy corn and that will be that. Imagine.

I tried to tell you everything I could think of.

Now stop eating my mom.

Warmly,

J.L.P.

One day, we will all be sea.

—Sun Yung Shin, *Unbearable Splendor*

Hi Deb. Hi. I wanted to wish you a Merry Christmas. And . . . I need to talk to Ted or somebody about cleaning the apartment. So if you will call me back when you can. Bye-bye.

Lone Star. Lone Ranger. Lone Survivor.

Lone Lone Lone

My Grandma Bonnie lives alone.

She snores very loudly.

She puts off doing her dishes until the next day.

If I ever saw my grandma with a smooth face it would startle me. I like her wiggly layers. She taught me how to swim in our lake by placing her hands under me, holding me up to the surface of the water, and then, very gently, letting me go.

When I called my grandma with the news that my marriage was falling apart, she told me that the day she found out my grandpa was sleeping with another woman she almost rammed her car into a tree. But she didn't do it because, she said, that would have been a stupid thing to do.

My grandma has one blue tooth. I have never asked her why; it just never occurred to me to question it. She had a knee replacement last year, and I drove home to be with her on the day of her surgery. I held her hand until the doctor came to put her under. We were laughing because earlier, on her way to the bathroom, she hadn't realized her gown was untied in the back. *I sure gave them all a show*, she said. As they wheeled her into surgery, I was thinking I might not see her again.

She has already chosen her funeral songs.

But this is not a story about my grandma. This is a story about Doris Ronn. Doris Ronn may be someone's grandma, but she's not my grandma. Doris Ronn calls my number often by mistake. She leaves messages on my voicemail, and I save them. Once, I was waiting to take my seat at a play reading when she called me for the third time that day. I had already explained to her that I am not Deb, that she is dialing the wrong number. Still, I go outside and dial her back.

Doris? I say.

Yes? she says. *This is Doris Ronn.*

Doris, you keep calling me, but I am not who you are looking for.

Well, that can't be, she says. *I have your number right here.*

And we go round and round like this.

The strange song sounded like a ghost at first. A low, moaning whisper at the bottom of the Puget Sound. Probably nothing. But maybe something. The classified sensors had been spread across the ocean floor by the Navy three years earlier. They were looking for Soviet submarines, but instead of submarines, they found a symphony. The ocean floor pulsing with noise. Aliveness. Oysters babbling. Tiny fish snapping the tendons of their pectoral fins. Contracting their bladder muscles. Showing off. Demanding attention. Battling for ground. Getting directions. Grunts and sighs and yelps and screams and songs and squeaks and murmurs and babbles. And then there was that whale. *Whoam Whoam Whoam.* A call of its own. Off the charts. Higher than high. The Mariah Carey of whales. One technician heard the recordings and took note.

This is Doris Ronn.

If you would call me or come in and see me, I would appreciate it.

"A unique whale call with 50–52 Hz emphasis from a single source has been tracked over 12 years in the central and eastern North Pacific. No other calls with similar characteristics have been identified in the acoustic data from any hydrophone system in the North Pacific basin. Only one series of these 52-Hz calls has been recorded at a time, with no call overlap, suggesting that a single whale produced the calls."

Marine biologist William A. Watkins spent the last years of his life tracking and researching the 52-Hz whale, otherwise known as *the loneliest whale on earth*. He followed the whale's call for twelve years. He never saw Whale. He only heard Whale.

Why wouldn't you show yourself, you lonely wailing animal?

I wonder how long she has been alone. I wonder if she watches *The Price Is Right* with the volume cranked way up. I wonder if she notices her creamer is spoiled. I wonder if she bathes. I wonder if she sweeps. I wonder if she wears a long nightgown to bed. I wonder if she ever sat doubled over on the toilet, suspecting a miscarriage. I wonder if her breasts still look like breasts. I wonder if her pubic hair has fallen off. I wonder if she misses dancing. I wonder if she knits white afghans for her great-grandchildren and pins notes to them with her full name, the date, and washing instructions on them. I wonder if she knows about the Internet. I wonder if her hands are gnarled into loose fists. I wonder if her chin sags. I wonder if she is afraid of falling because her best friend spent an entire night face-down on her kitchen floor and her body was cold when the downstairs neighbor found her. I wonder if her husband ever called her a *Fat Ass*, if he died from complications related to smoking. I wonder if he wore an oxygen tank for nine years, if she brought him a tray of raw onion slices and bologna and crackers every afternoon while he slowly suffocated. I wonder if she was quietly relieved when he finally died. I wonder if she does sudoku, writes birthday cards, bakes banana bread. I wonder if she has dreams where she is flying, swooping through trees, zooming past buildings, if she wakes up with a gasp every time she flies downward, just before hitting the ground.

Deb? Is that you? . . . Deb? . . . I'm calling you.

A List of Whale Facts

1. The blue whale is one of the loudest animals on earth.

2. Their calls can be heard underwater for hundreds of miles.

3. Calls last anywhere from five to thirty minutes.

4. Calls often repeat themselves.

5. Blue whales call for long periods of time after losing a member of their pod.

6. Some researchers say whales cannot feel sad because whales are not human.

7. The call of a normal blue whale is 10 to 40 Hz.

8. If a whale's call is 52 Hz, other whales most likely cannot hear it.

9. If other whales cannot hear it, that whale will be very alone.

10. If that whale is very alone, this seems very sad.

11. If this seems very sad, this is very sad.

Hi Deb. This is Doris Ronn. Um . . . I just wanted to say hi to you. And . . .

My grandma was slowly going blind in one of her eyes. She did not tell anyone about this. She did not want us to worry. Instead, she got herself up in the middle of the night to practice playing her piano in the dark. *Just to see if I could still play*, is what she said.

But this is not a story about my grandma. This is a story about Doris Ronn. It has been five months since I've heard from Doris Ronn, and I'm starting to wonder where she went. I think of calling, just to check in, but something stops me.

Doris Ronn heard a sound while she lay awake in bed one night. At first, she wondered if she was dreaming. It was a low sound. A soft sound. Haunting almost. Barely audible.

Whoam Whoam Whoam

The sound throbbed so softly she felt it in the back of her throat. It vibrated into her, this lonely tuba sound. It whirred in a beautiful, deep melody. Like a cat purring on her throat, she could feel this. She wondered if her hearing aid was acting up. She had recently gotten a new one at Sam's Club and had been having trouble with the background noise being too loud. But when she put her finger to her ear to feel for it, it wasn't there. She felt for her glasses, pushed herself slowly onto her elbows, and clicked on the bedside lamp. Nothing was there. The mattress dampened in a warm pool beneath her. She was scared, but also ready. She had been waiting for this.

It was four in the morning, and my grandma thought she would get up and make herself some peanut butter crackers with honey. But what happened was that she ended up on her bedroom floor, unable to stand. She felt very strange. Everything wobbled. The chair, the dresser, everything. She felt as if she were floating. *This is it*, she thought. She crawled to her kitchen on her hands and knees and banged on the floor with the handle of a broom.

This kind of an ending is just not fair. All of her smiling, all of her music. Shouldn't it all end with twirling or at least a graceful bow? I didn't even lay awake in bed, feeling something was off. She pounded and pounded.

Over the years, Doris Ronn's body had sorted itself into an arrange-
ment of brittle bones and sagging skin that tried to look like her, but
it wasn't. It wasn't her at all. She could see a flaking scalp through
white tufts of matted hair, feel arms hanging knobbed like sticks at
her sides. It amazed her that she could make those arms move, being
that they weren't even hers. She had been asking around a lot lately.
Stopping people in the hallway of her apartment building. Trying to
find out what had happened to herself. *Do you know where I went?* She
would ask the mailman, the dog walker, the pock-faced teenager col-
lecting carts in the grocery store parking lot. Their reaction was always the same. Raised eyebrows. A soft chuckle. *Why won't you help
me?* She would shout at them. She was growing tired of averted eyes,
tired of searching for herself. So she began to wait for her ending.

Doris Ronn did not bother with the mattress, she somehow knew she
wouldn't be back. And anyway, the idea of letting the wet be excited
her. She pulled on the frayed blue robe that hung on the back of her
bedroom door. She suddenly felt more alive, wrapped in blue like this.
The throbbing sound grew louder, more urgent, and she let it fill her

now. She even began to hum along playfully, to match the tone with her own voice. She slipped her gnarled feet into her Crocs, made her way to the front door and walked out. The sound was a call now, she knew that, and she knew she had to follow it.

She took the elevator down to the dimly lit first floor and walked past the receptionist who was asleep with her face on the desk. She passed the solarium with all those sleeping parakeets, walked out the double doors and into the salty night air. Because it was the middle of the night, there were no cars to worry about, and she crossed the street as quickly as the feet that didn't belong to her would allow. She hadn't walked this fast in years. She made her way across the board-walk and paused as cool sand filled her shoes. She should be colder, wearing only a nightgown and a thin blue robe, but the sound in her ears and in the back of her throat warmed her from the inside, as if she had swallowed a small piece of sun.

At first, when I realize she has taken her hands away, I feel myself begin to sink. *I cannot do this alone.* My small body takes on more water, and I'm sure I will be swallowed. But then I look up, and I think I can see her wrinkled neck stretched tight against the sky. She is laughing, her blue tooth peeking out from under her tongue like a secret jewel.

I close my eyes and let myself float.

One reason why whales breach is to quickly transmit information such as location.

The sky was black and piled with stars. Small waves caressed her hairless ankles, pulling sand from underneath her feet, beckoning her. Not too far from the beach where she stood, but far enough for great deepness, she saw the glistening giant shoot straight out of the water — a writhing, slick submarine meeting surface in a fantastic explosion of water and whale. She reacted normally, as if she were merely seeing a bus stopping at a stoplight. Her eyes would not leave the spot where it had met water. She felt a kind of primordial softness toward this creature, as if they had once swung together on a swing set or they shared the same birthday. Immediately, Doris Ronn knew that this was her caller. She was really far away from her apartment, from her television, from the leftover rotisserie chicken in her refrigerator. She was really going somewhere now. She enjoyed the feeling of something wanting her this badly, the feeling of being pulled further and further in.

It was her inner ear. Peripheral vestibular disorder. That is what was causing her to feel like she was floating. I heard about it three days later and I cried and cried because no one had even thought to call me. While sitting on my kitchen floor leaning my back against the refrigerator I thought how silly I was being. It was just an ear problem. She was okay. As she told me the whole story on the phone I could hear *The Young and the Restless* blaring in the background. My grandma even laughed about the whole thing.

I'm just falling apart, Sweetheart.

The call was louder than ever now, it crowded her ears and filled her throat and the backs of her eyelids with its heavy pulse. She called back in harmony, rising a third above, right where her voice was at its most colorful. Deep under the water, she found that she hardly even missed breathing.

The whale waited. He wasn't worried about being found. He was bigger than the biggest dinosaur that ever lived, a floating ghost giant. He was both the shadow of the building and the building. And he was used to waiting.

The great pulling stopped and her white hair swirled around face her like seagrass. This was the moment in her life when Doris Ronn could have been mistaken for a mermaid. It was there under the surface of the ocean, wrapped tight in wet blue, that the two callers finally met face to face. One was creature. The other was person. It doesn't matter which was which. If a smile had a sound, that is the sound they both made.

This is not the sad part, so do not look away.

The salt would work quickly on the body that didn't belong to Doris Ronn, undressing her layer by layer, until all that was left was soft light wrapped in blue robe. It was no coincidence that her caller was also blue, that the ocean that cradled them both was blue. Blue is a very good ending to things.

Recently, sensors off the coast of California picked up whale calls with the same frequency as the 52-Hz whale. The recordings suggest that there is now more than one whale with a uniquely high-pitched call.

We only see them when they come up for air.

ACKNOWLEDGMENTS

My heartfelt thanks to those who made this book possible: to my editors at *Seneca Review Books*, Geoffrey Babbitt and David Weiss, for believing in my manuscript, and to Jenny Boully, for her generosity and kindness. To my fierce and brilliant writing professors at Hamline University: Deborah Keenan, Patricia Weaver Francisco, Juliet Patterson, and Angela Pelster-Wiebe—thank you for helping me get a grip and hone my weirdness, for saying that imagination and the essay belong together, for letting me bring eggs and flying squirrels to class. Thank you to Jessie Rae Rayle and Katie Vyvyan, for their unwavering friendship. To my sister, Jenny, for giving me bloody noses, for making me stronger. I am grateful to my beloved grandma, for her inexhaustible love, for bravely letting me write about her. Thank you to my mom and dad, for plopping me into the woods early on.

Thank you to Doris Ronn, wherever you are.

To my fellow creatures whom I have lived with, ridden on, dreamt about and held while dying, this place is truly yours.

Thank you to Westin and Winter, my wildest dreams. And thank you, Jason, for being with me while I dug and dug.

NOTES

"BEAUTIFUL WEATHERS"

This essay is a collage comprised of existing work from famous literary giants, personal heroes, as well as books that I have not read. Thanks to: Elizabeth Alexander, John Brandon, Joan Didion, Annie Dillard, Montaigne, Jim Moore, Tim O'Brien, Angela Pelster, Joe Sacco, Jeannette Walls, and James Wright. Montaigne is responsible for *shit*; please direct all complaints to France. There is a line in John Brandon's *A Million Heavens* about an uncle having to take something like an uncle that did not make it. It was not weather-related.

"THIS IS DORIS RONN"

P. 70: William A. Watkins, "Twelve Years of Tracking 52-Hz Whale Calls from a Unique Source in the North Pacific," http://www.sciencedirect.com/science/article/pii/S0967063704001682.

ABOUT THE AUTHOR

Jessica Lind Peterson is an essayist, playwright, and theatre artist. Her essays have appeared in *Orion*, *Seneca Review*, *River Teeth*, *Passages North*, *Alaska Quarterly Review*, and others. She is also co-founder of a little theatre called Yellow Tree, and holds an MFA in Creative Writing from Hamline University in St. Paul. She lives with her family in Canyon, Minnesota in a trailer that is painted green.